How to Get a New Identity & Disappear

The Right Way

by Tristan Trubble

Published in USA by:

Tristan Trubble
P.O BOX #9
Boynton Beach
FL 33425

© Copyright 2016

ISBN-13: 978-1540314062
ISBN-10: 1540314065

ALL RIGHTS RESERVED. No part of this publication may be reproduced or transmitted in any form whatsoever, electronic, or mechanical, including photocopying, recording, or by any informational storage or retrieval system without express written, dated and signed permission from the author.

Table of Contents

Why You Might Need a New Identity 1

Legal vs. Illegal 6

Using the System to Your Advantage 12

Paying Attention to the Particulars 21

Using Your New Identity in the Real World 28

Things You Need to Consider 33

Areas & Obstacles to Avoid 39

Leaving Your Past Behind 45

Why You Might Need a New Identity

Almost everybody, at some point or another, considers what it would be like to have a new identity. Some of us simply daydream about having a "Do Over" button, a device that would allow us to go back in time and start over, while others have a more vivid imagination and would like to assume the role of super spy, capable of infiltrating society using multiple identities to hide who we really are.

The majority of us never act on our ambitions in the new identity retrieval process, primarily because of the risks involved. In most countries and states it is illegal to obtain a new identity without implementing the proper legal procedures established by the government.

Having a new identity can open several doors and opportunities to a person that had previously encountered difficulty in a specific area of interest. Individuals that have a criminal record containing a multitude of felony charges often seek ways to abolish their current existence and manufacture a new one. In many states people that have felony or criminal records encounter increased difficulty when applying for a job, attempting to purchase a weapon, or registering to vote. They may even be subject to constant reporting of their physical location if the nature of their offense involves a sex crime. While most people convicted of a felony are guilty of the charges they receive, the judicial system does not always work as it should; nor does it differentiate or detail the nature of the offense when making personal information public regarding those that have been labeled with sex offender status. An 18 year old male that sleeps with his 17 year old girlfriend can be charged with Statutory Rape. They can also be subject to the same identical sex offender status as a 50 year old child molester. The two events are drastically different from one another yet the general internet searching public is not made aware of the particulars surrounding the case. The social dogma associated with being identified in this category can be extremely damaging and rather unfair to the 18 year old who acted on desire and impulse.

There are others that simply want to escape the humdrum boring life they have ended up in. They are unhappy with the current path they are taking through life and would like to invent a more interesting person. Maybe they have been allowing one or both of their parents to live vicariously through them for a number of years. Perhaps they were intimidated into toiling away in a career field that was chosen for them as part of the family tradition that they would like to leave behind now that the parents have passed away.

A handful of individuals specialize in producing a myriad of multiple identities in order to conduct con games or schemes. In this day and age the average consumer has become attuned to ensuring the identities of those they elect to conduct business with. Unscrupulous sales people that are looking to make a buck by promoting a product they know to be useless or fake will use false identification techniques in order to make the sale and keep from being held liable.

There are legitimate as well as illegitimate reasons that people entertain the idea of seeking a new method by which they can identify themselves. Witnessing a major crime and providing significant testimony might lead a concerned citizen to try and create a new image for them and their families as a protective measure.

Having a terrible or less than average credit rating will also lead some individuals down the path to obtaining an identity with less baggage attached to it. Several industries in the modern era use personal credit ratings and scores of potential clients to establish a basis for conducting business with a person, even if it has absolutely nothing to do with the nature of their business. Insurance companies of all kinds request this information from their prospects even though a person's credit rating bears no weight on how well that person takes care of the possessions they want to protect through insurance.

You might find it necessary to change who people think you are in order to receive more favorable decisions from institutions that view credit history as the ultimate deciding factor employed for approving your application.

Depending on the nature of your business or career you might find a new name a valuable commodity to have available to protect your true identity. Authors often invent pen names for pieces of literature they do not want related to the identity they use for other works of art. They may do this to keep from damaging the reputation they have established under their original name. One such famous author chose to write several books under a pen name simply to see if his audience was purchasing his novels based on name recognition alone or if they were purchasing the material due to their enjoyment of the story being told.

Hollywood actors and movie stars, as well as mega-moguls in the music industry often establish a stage name or new identity by which their fans can associate their music with them. They use this stage name everywhere they go and in some cases never divulge their given name to anyone but those that are within their trusted circle. They use these new identities to their advantage and create corporations under the banner in order to enjoy the things they couldn't prior to becoming famous. This alter ego affords them the respect of immediate recognition and opens doors that would otherwise remain sealed shut. Without these stage names in place they would have to rely on their given name and associated life events to obtain the things they require in order to maintain a successful career.

You need to consider all of the reasons and possible ramifications of obtaining a new image and applicable name before making the decision to proceed with the process. Living a lifestyle under more than one name can open several doors of opportunity, yet it can permanently seal other doors that might have been advantageous or beneficial had you elected to remain intact as your true self.

As with anything of this nature there can be severe and stiff penalties associated with obtaining an eminence front. If you are looking to fall off the proverbial radar, then it may not matter to you which method you use to get the credentials you will find necessary. That being said, if you have a legitimate reason for wanting an alternative identity, then it is highly recommended you seek professional and legal assistance in this area as it will be more beneficial and legitimate in the long run.

Legal vs. Illegal

There are basically two ways to go about getting the paperwork you will need to promote your new persona. As indicated above you can elect to use legal methods for procuring the proper legal documentation, or you can eliminate the hassle and go it alone.

Legally altering your image for protective purposes is usually fairly easy to accomplish. You should contact a legal expert in the field for further consultation. It will be important to discover what information you might need in order to hasten the event and secure your new social security number, birth certificate and image enhanced ID cards, such as a Driver's License, Passport or state issued ID. Depending on the nature of the circumstances you may have to go before a court and explain your case to the judge before being granted permission to proceed. Once you have the proper paperwork in place and have been granted approval by the governing body the rest of the state agencies will accept the documentation and make the appropriate changes.

While obtaining a new identification legally may seem the most secure route to take that is not always the case. Keep in mind that the people present during the process are all susceptible to corrupt practices. They may perform the proper procedures as part of their professional career position; however they may inadvertently or purposely divulge pertinent information to another that can result in the new you being discovered by the very people or person you were trying to avoid.

Within the illegal field of alter ego invention a concerned citizen has two choices available to them. They can elect to employ the assistance of another individual that specializes in producing illegal paperwork that appears authentic or they can go it alone and use intuition and imagination to secure the articles of importance associated with this type of endeavor.

Believe it or not, the majority of us know someone or an associate of someone that is proficient in this area, whether we realize it or not. People that are effective and efficient at printing off legitimate looking paperwork normally keep a very low profile. They are providing a service that policing agencies view as criminal and detrimental. You may have to do a little research among known and trusted affiliates before discovering who this person is. You will not find an advertisement in a community directory for people of this nature.

Keep in mind that using this method also involves the risk of possible exposure. While these individuals do not maintain records regarding the people they have supplied with a new ID, they do tend to remember faces of clients that come to them for this purpose. If they are placed in an unfavorable position by a law enforcement agency or criminal entity they may divulge the secrets they were supposed to keep and let the cat out of the bag so to speak. They are no different than you or I, their personal preservation is going to be foremost in their mind should they be faced with possible persecution or life threatening situations.

Attempting to obtain an entirely new image can be a rather easy process to accomplish by those that have the insight, ingenuity and relative knowledge about the process. As you can imagine, showing up at the local DMV to ask for new identifying documents without an initial piece of accepted paperwork is going to be impossible.

If it were that simple you wouldn't know who your neighbors really were since we would all be living in a comic book environment full of heroes, villains and super sleuths. You need to know what it is you are getting into before you decide on a name and location for yourself. Make no mistake about it, if you do not use the proper precautions, your new identity may end up being far worse than your previous one. The last thing you want to do is invent an image for yourself that is associated with a name that has more baggage attached to it than the one you are trying to abolish or eliminate.

When performed correctly and successfully the illegitimacy of a new ID should only be known to one person, that person being you. Under certain circumstances, such as being implemented in a Witness Protection Program it may be necessary to involve the immediate members of the family; however the fewer people involved with the process, the greater chances of success you can expect.

You might want to consider a complete upheaval of the norm in your efforts. If you currently enjoy living life in the lap of luxury, then you should probably search for a new residence in a rural region of the world. Places with smaller populations are easier to assess and monitor than metropolitan areas, especially if you are successful at blending into the surroundings and making a new name for yourself. Small town communities take care of their own constituents a little better than locales where an abundance of individuals gravitate. You have a far better chance of being alerted should your false identity be discovered in a small town environment than you do in a major city.

The primary purpose of getting a new name for yourself is to remain incognito. Keep this in mind as you may have to change some of your societal habits in order to maintain the integrity of the ruse. You might find it beneficial to change the type of people you associate with. Nothing will tip off the curious more than the continuation of a creature of habit. In other words if your present persona likes to visit the local gang affiliated watering hole for several shots of spirits you may want to eliminate this event from your community calendar. Those that might be looking for you will begin their search in the areas they know you to be familiar with. If you were previously considered a blemish on society in your last community you might want to consider becoming noticed in more favorable environments, consider attending a church, or taking an interest in an area you would have otherwise avoided like the plague. Reinventing your image does not stop at getting new identifying documents.

Depending on the circumstances that resulted in you deciding to approach the opportunity of obtaining this new image, it may also be important to consider the lives of those you are leaving behind. In order for a new identity to be successful and effective you may have to completely obliterate any relationships you had prior to taking on this new persona. This can include immediate as well as extended family members as well as friends and associates. If you are running and hiding from something, those you leave behind may bear the brunt of your decision should those hunting for you elect to involve them or their lives.

   http://www.bombshock.com/fake_id/how_to_create_a_new_indentity.html is a very useful resource worth investigating.

Using the System to Your Advantage

It is important to note that the information described here is for entertainment and educational purposes only. It should in no way be considered a suggested practice or recommendation for those looking to alleviate or eliminate possible punishment from prosecution.

One of the easiest ways to begin the process of securing documents to support your new identity is by using the same system put in place to prevent such activities from occurring. Scanning the obituaries of several newspapers around the country will be the diving board from which you want to launch a persona changing plunge. Obituaries contain legally accepted and established names of those that have recently passed away. The government agencies assigned to provide identification for the living are also responsible for recording the names of the recently deceased. In most cases this procedure is neglected or performed inappropriately, thereby leaving ample and useful information available to anyone wanting to reinvent themselves. The record keeping procedures these agencies employ are seriously lacking in a majority of states and cities. They do not advertise this flaw for the simple fact it would entice criminal minded citizens to circumvent the laws they are trying to enforce.

All you need is one good piece of false ID in order to complete the dismantling and reconstruction of your image. The obituaries will not only provide you with a name, they will also provide you with a date of birth which is going to be extremely important when applying for the new documents you desire. Once you have the new name you want to use and a date of birth for the person, you can try to place a simple inquisitive phone call. For this step of the process it may be better to search obituaries listed in major metropolitan news media. Not only are there more selections to choose from, but you run less risk of someone at the county office recognizing the name of the decedent and complicating matters. Small towns and cities have fewer listings on average and therefore may employ better record keeping methods and statistics for their region. County offices and the employees that staff them in major cities promote a more lackadaisical atmosphere to following protocol; the names of the deceased are seldom given the attention they deserve. It is from these listings of the less fortunate you will find the right name for your new image.

Do not, under any circumstances, assume that

blindly choosing a name and date of birth is going to provide the results you have in mind. You will still need to conduct a little more research. You do not want to make a new name for yourself using the identity of a recently deceased 88 year old community icon. You will need to dig a little deeper and determine how old the person was when they passed. It will be more beneficial and believable if your selection for this situation has an age relative to your own. It doesn't have to be an exact match, just try to keep the difference in age to a minimum. A good rule of thumb to employ for this procedure is to maintain a +/- ratio of five years, especially for those at middle or aged advanced stages of life.

You will also want to learn a little bit about the person in question before going forward. How popular were they in the community? Are they having an enormous funeral attended by dozens or hundreds of people, or did their obituary only contain two to three lines indicating little is known about next of kin? The harder it is to find out information about a prospective person, the more likely it is they will be a good match for your image altering efforts.

That is not all you will want to know about the person or identity you plan on assuming. You will also want to ensure they do not have harmful baggage exceeding that which you are trying to get rid of. It will not do you any good to manufacture a new existence for yourself if the person you pick has a catastrophic credit history, or has a criminal record so long it can't be read in a single sitting. You may end up finding yourself in far greater trouble than you had bargained for. The picture perfect candidate will be one that very few people knew on a personal level. Look for the basic, garden variety, John Doe obituary with an actual name. Single, loner types are the best resource for this endeavor.

    You can search the internet for additional information of the criminal nature. If the individual has a lengthy history or possible warrants in waiting cross them off your list and continue. Discovering a person's current credit history can be a little more difficult, especially if a social security number is not determined or available. Credit reporting companies are very adept at record keeping and maintenance; they will not divulge the necessary information to anyone without the proper credentials. Fortunately there are other ways to get a feeling for how well the decedent kept their credit rating. You can place a courtesy call to a utility provider in the area explaining that you are a distant relative of the individual and that you were hoping to make accommodations for shutting off their services and paying the final bill. In most cases the utility provider will not ask for positive proof of your identity or relationship to the account and will provide you with the amount of the final bill. If these are months past due it is probably safe to assume that the person has a less than desirable credit history and should be eliminated.

Once you have narrowed down the field of selection and chosen an identity to assume, you will need to put on your best theater mask and perform for the proper audience. The next step of the process will involve placing another phone call to the county office where the person was born. This is very important to remember, since the place of birth is the ONLY party responsible for issuing a new birth certificate. Find out where the deceased was born, where they passed away is only important in alerting you to the one location on Earth you do not want to relocate to. Call the county office and get in touch with the right person. Offer an explanation that is believable for obtaining the new birth certificate. Something such as, "Hello, my name is _____, I was born in _____ County on __/__/__. I have been living abroad in _____ as a missionary for the last 15 years, during which time I suffered the loss of all my personal possessions. I was wondering if you could assist me in getting a copy of my birth certificate."

Be on your toes and prepared to answer any questions they might ask with confidence. Do not hem and haw searching for the right thing to say when you are on the phone. They may ask for your social security number, something they assume everyone should immediately know. Explain this away. As a missionary you did not have a use for your social security card, it has been 15 years since anyone asked for it and you can't for the life of you recall what it was. Give them the first three digits it might have been. Social Security numbers are assigned to a person by region of residence at the time of applying or being assigned one. The first three digits identify the state or region within a state where the card was issued. For instance, in the state of Hawai'i residents often have an SSN that begins with '576', it's like an area code for the card, so if you can utter off the first three digits they are familiar with, it may be enough for them to consider you a little more legitimate.

They might ask for your place of birth, as in which hospital you were delivered at. Research and familiarize yourself with what was available in the area 15 years ago, the time at which you supposedly became a missionary.

Nothing will send off flares and warning signs like insisting you were born at a regional facility that has only been in existence for the last five years. You have to have a salesman's mentality to overcome some of these obstacles. Listen, react and respond with confidence. Explain that you are not entirely confident about which hospital you were delivered in. You might attempt to offer an explanation that alludes to the fact your parents passed away at an early age and you were sent off to live with relatives who were unable to provide you with this vital data.

The names of the parents of the new persona you are trying to assume will be available to the person on the other end of the phone as they will be present on the birth certificate. This is the most difficult obstacle to overcome should it arise. The only believable explanation for not knowing the names of your parents involves being adopted, and unless this occurred through human trafficking on the black market, very few are going to buy a bogus excuse. Sometimes this information may be available in the obituary. Pay attention to detail; if the obit indicated the deceased was preceded in death by parents and/or siblings jot down those names, they will come in handy. You will not only be able to give the names of the parents but also rattle off the names of your siblings for further verification.

Be aware of every aspect associated with this exercise in procuring the new you. The person on the other end of the phone has absolutely no idea who they are talking to. Establish a professional attitude, atmosphere and rapport. You are selling an idea. This person needs to feel as if they are the only lifeline you have available for establishing who you are. Make them your friend, keep your temper in check, and make reasonable requests that appear to result from dire circumstances, eliminate making demands or ill advised requests to speak with a supervisor. People in the human resources service industry like to feel important and needed. They face an abundance of verbal abuse on a daily basis which tends to set the tone by which they function and operate. Turn the tables for a change and give them a breath of fresh air. Become the reason that they smile the rest of the day even though they are bombarded with insults aimed at causing injury.

You have to control the flow of the conversation. The easiest way to build confidence and trust and initiate a friendship is by getting the other person to talk about themselves. Use your "missionary" experiences to get them involved with the communication process, find a common thread that lets them relate a story of their own, identify with it, relate back to it, use it to your advantage. The more comfortable they are speaking with you the more open they will become to ultimately helping you out.

Do not use this information unwisely. If you call a county office to request a new birth certificate for an identity you would like to assume as your own from a region or area within accessible driving distance from your current location you are going to fail miserably. County offices that issue these documents normally require you to appear in person to receive the copy. Make sure this would pose a serious inconvenience for you to accommodate. Live in Florida, shop in Oregon.

For those that would like to use an internet based service for securing the documents they require I recommend visiting http://www.espionage-store.com/newidentityletter.html and researching and investigating what they have to offer.

Paying Attention to the Particulars

The brand new birth certificate is not the end of the new identity line. You will also need a new Social Security card, a new driver's license and maybe even a new passport. Laws regarding the issuance of social security cards have changed over the decades. In the not too distant past a person was not issued an SSN until such a time as they were considered of legal age to work or pay taxes. In today's society the majority of American citizens are issued an SSN at birth. This change will be important for procuring the new SSN card. If the individual serving as your deceased doppelganger was born prior to 1986 chances are they were not issued an SSN at birth, which will be more advantageous to you in the long run. It can explain why you do not recall the number or why the first three digits you offer do not coincide with the ones that were in place at the suspected time of issuance.

You can also use this information to apply for a new SSN card, especially if the name chosen happens to incorporate a common surname. The SSN agency will attempt to track down any existing number associated with the name and relevant information they are provided. They will want to see the birth certificate before producing a new number. You may be able to explain that due to your religious beliefs and missionary path you chose directly out of high school you were never issued an SSN. If they discover one issued by a specific state you can insist you never lived in that area, it will be near impossible and exhausting for them to try and prove otherwise. Deny, deny, and deny any and all scenarios that could prevent them from producing the documentation you desire, if they are not going to assist you they do not need to be alerted to your efforts.

You will also need a new driver's license. Getting this will also require two forms of verifiable identification in most states. The birth certificate and SSN will suffice; however you will have to check with local regulations with your DMV to discover any other avenues of opportunity for providing acceptable paperwork. Avoid attempting to circumvent the necessary procedures for applying for a driver's license since this agency has a greater tendency to follow guidelines and procedures than do others. Your appearance at the DMV with little or no proof is going to increase the amount of scrutiny they approach you with when you return.

Most people want a new identity in order to escape a problematic past of some nature. In order to accomplish this you will need to keep and maintain a very low profile. You might want to avoid trying to establish a new credit history as far as procuring plastic is concerned. If you pay in cash you have less chance of establishing recordable data that can be used to discover your true identity.

Modern technology has made it easier to get the things you need in order to establish a new identity. That being said it has also made it easier for others to investigate and determine the authenticity of an identifying document.

Know what you are getting into before you take the first step. Do the homework and research required that will allow you to be successful the first time around. Government agencies often communicate with one another even if they do not track and record statistics and vital information as they should. If you draw attention to yourself in one agency, it may have far and wide spread effects that prevent you from taking further action. Consider every possible action and reaction to an unexpected scenario. With the tools private and public citizens have at their disposal it would not be unheard of for an issuing entity to request photographic proof in the form of a time stamped and dated depiction of your physical appearance. Do not be afraid to claim technological ignorance as an excuse for not being able to meet their demands. Even in this day and age the internet is not readily available to all citizens, especially those in rural areas.

The same rules apply to securing a new passport that supports your eminence front. These documents are provided by the federal government and are subject to intense investigative procedures. If you do not need a passport, then eliminate it from your endeavor at all costs. You are more likely to get caught trying to flee federal charges by attempting to obtain a passport then you are by finding a nice quiet little church mouse community to spend the rest of your days in. You only need so much identification to succeed in life and live comfortably. Avoid being obvious or drawing unwanted attention to your efforts of remaining incognito.

Involve as few outside resources in the form of friends and family as possible. If they know what you are doing, where you are headed, and what new name to call you by, it may be enough to expose the entire scam. The new identification numbers you are trying to obtain will be provided by a local, state or federal prison system rather than a regular agency. This will also apply to the employees of the agency you contact for each piece of identification. Ask for the name of the person assigned to assist you, write it down along with which agency they are associated with. If you have to make more than one call or visit, insist on seeing the same case worker.

The fewer eyes that fall across your information the better off you will be. Haphazard habits that allow anyone in the agency to look over your info can result in complete catastrophe.

Even if you are successful in your efforts to obtain a new identity it would be wise to invent a nickname to go along with the masquerade. Trust will be a commodity you can no longer afford under the best of circumstances. Once you begin living a lie and people around you start to buy into it, they are not going to take kindly to being informed they fell for a lie. They will turn on you in a heartbeat regardless of how much they invested in establishing a relationship with you.

Get familiar with using and answering to the new name. Nothing will cause curiosity or draw the attention of the astute like a person that doesn't seem to know their name. You might want to develop the habit of answering to everything or ignoring every comment tossed in your direction as a way of explaining away any nuances.

They say old habits are hard to break. It can also be said that old habits are hard to fake. Establishing an alternate identity that is believable will require appearing as though you know what you are doing. It will not only be important to develop new habits, it will be extremely imperative to look as if you have been doing these things all your life. You don't want to apply for a position at an Oil Change facility if you are going to be constantly manicuring your fingernails.

Avoid making routines or abiding by revolving schedules. Alter where you go and how you get there whenever possible. Not everyone can exist or blend into a small town community; some will still prefer the atmosphere of the big city. If this applies to you, then consider relocating continuously. Find an out of the way place to hang your hat for a few months and then move on.

I've found http://www.espionage-store.com/newidentityletter.html to be a very worthwhile website for investigating opportunities to change your identity successfully.

Using Your New Identity in the Real World

How you decide to use your new identity in the real world environment is completely up to you. The majority of people in this position would like to maintain as low a profile as possible. All your new identity has to do is provide you with enough means to survive. Identity hopping from one persona to another to escape credit card responsibilities is eventually going to get you caught. If you are going to establish a new line of credit in conjunction with your new identity, then make sure you use better shopping and reimbursement habits. Only use the cards when absolutely necessary, to make reservations for temporary accommodations or things of that nature. Pay with cash whenever possible and avoid using the credit cards or debit cards for average every day purchases, especially if some of your current habits are similar to the ones you were supposed to leave behind.

Yes, having a new identity can be very rewarding; it can also be very cumbersome and complex. The old you had very little to be concerned with when asked to provide proper identification in the past. You more than likely were forced into establishing a habit of carrying around your ID card and providing it whenever asked. The new you will need to ask yourself why it is necessary to divulge personal and private information before absent mindedly handing over something to prove your existence. Always be cautious with disclosure. Depending on the level of secrecy you would like to enjoy you may find it advantageous to use the identity of associates to secure the necessities you need on a daily basis such as utilities. If you can find a rental residence with everything included for one monthly cost that will help you maintain a covert and concealed atmosphere to your efforts.

Make the most out of your new identity but do so methodically and with moderation. Don't try to go overboard all at once and apply for and obtain ridiculous loans for unnecessary adventures. If you really want to masquerade your true identity you need to appear as though you just fell out of the sky one day with no forewarning. Start from scratch and keep it low and slow. Your current credit history should appear as though it took several years to establish, even if you have the financial means available to max out a piece of plastic one day and pay it off the next. Obtain the creature comforts you can live with over the course of time. Keep in mind you didn't win the lottery, just a new lease on life.

Do not under any circumstances use your new identity to conduct business with the life or loved ones you left behind, especially if your survival directly depends on them remaining uneducated about your current existence. Anything out of the ordinary will cause watchful eyes to notice the action. The new you needs to focus on the future and forget about the past. You cannot expect to remain a well-guarded secret if you are causing abnormal behavior in those you are trying to protect. Even if they are unaware you are still alive, they can be exposed to risk.

Confidence is going to be the key factor to success in the new identity industry. Your masquerade will be played out in front of people you have never met. Any cracks, crevices or chinks in the armor will be magnified under most circumstances. The past history of your new identity will also need to be fabricated with care and caution. Each and every time you tell a new acquaintance a story about where you have been or what you have done it will need to flow with other information that has already been made available.

Develop a punctual and plausible timeline of past events. Do not deviate or embellish the details with every additional telling of the story. Keep it simple. Simple is boring. Boring stories result in less investigative enthusiasm on behalf of the inquirer. Simple leads to boredom, boredom leads to safety and security. Nobody cares much if you spent the last 15 years digging irrigation and drainage ditches for the Department of Transportation out in sunny California. They will however want to pick your brain if you come across as being an important and influential individual that has traveled the world.

Cover your tracks when applying your new identity in the real world. Never allude to having been involved in an important or well-documented event. If you indicate having earned a degree from a specific institution of higher learning be prepared for it to be verified, even if it does not apply to anything you are doing in your new life. Nosy neighbors reside in every region of the world. What you think might be unimportant in a general piece of conversation could lead to your undoing. Keep your cards up your sleeve and never tip your hat, even if the old you did participate in a specific event or enjoy a relevant experience firsthand, the new you was elsewhere and should not develop misplaced recollection.

Limit the number of people you socialize with as well as the information you disburse. Strangers are friends you haven't met yet; however friends are also known enemies. If you let someone into your inner trust circle, you expose the risk of being turned out to the community. Your substitute identity should be so well planned and played out that the stone carver puts your fake name on the tombstone.

Once you have completed the process of obtaining legitimate looking false identification documents, you may want to repeat the process and even have a new location set up and waiting for your arrival. If you do become discovered you can vanish overnight without enduring the same lengthy process. Having a second and separate false ID may also be useful for traveling purposes should you elect to venture out beyond your established comfort zone. If this will apply to you and your efforts, then showing up at a new location for business or pleasure under the guise of another completely different persona will assist you in covering your tracks. Nobody will associate your traveling identity with the one you use at your home base of operations.

If you are going to be constantly and consistently relocating as part of the new persona plan then you will want to obtain as many new identities as possible and use a different one for every new venture. Even if the previous doppelganger disguise was a resounding success you should avoid using it in back to back scenarios. If somebody shows up at the last community looking for you the trail will go cold once they try and pick it back up on their way out of town.

Things You Need to Consider

Before making the decision to drop off the face of the Earth and establish a new identity you need to consider a few things first. What are you trying to run from? Are you in legal trouble? Are you facing a criminal charge that carries a prison sentence as part of the penalty? Who will your disappearance adversely affect? Are you leaving behind children, a wife, parents, siblings, friends and/or business associates? Has your life or the life of your loved ones been threatened? Will starting a new life really provide you with a better lifestyle or is it going to complicate matters for everyone involved? Are you prepared to completely and entirely leave behind everything in your past temporarily or permanently?

These are but a handful of concerns that should cross the mind of anyone considering designing a new identity. What are the effects of your actions going to have on others? Let's say you are facing criminal charges with severe consequences in the form of sentencing. You more than likely had to be bonded out of jail while you await trial. In most cases a family member has to put up something of sizeable collateral to secure the bond amount for your release. If you skip town and cannot be found the bonding agency is not going to have any leniency on the family member or collateral that was offered as compensation. Your family member could end up losing their house, vehicle or other valued possession. Allowing them to suffer for your irresponsible behavior isn't going to paint a warm "Welcome Home," banner for the future.

How will your disappearance affect the emotional state of those you leave behind? When you suddenly vanish without forewarning the friends and family members you left behind will go through a period of grieving without closure. You will be leaving them with an open grave so to speak. It can create wide spread and devastating turmoil within the remaining family dynamics. Your actions may cause others you trust, love and hold dear to undergo mental as well as emotional counseling in order to cope with the unexplained and unexpected loss. The people you leave in the past will undoubtedly spare no expense in trying to locate you or find out what happened. All of these financial expenditures will come from their own personal savings and any donations they can procure through community funded support programs. Is it really going to be worth running away if your family has to suffer through these types of scenarios?

In addition to the impact it is going to have on others, stop and think for a second how it is going to affect you. Immediate and distant relocation is going to be necessary. Your current and existing lifestyle is going to have to be a long forgotten foggy memory. If you are transferring to a foreign location then learning the native language is going to be beneficial. Researching and discovering native traditions and tendencies will also be something you want to consider. The more in tune you are with your new surroundings the less likely you are to stand out like a sore thumb.

What will you do for work? How will you support yourself? Chances are if you are living under an eminence front you do not have the financial resources at your disposal to support yourself comfortably for the rest of your life. You will need to learn a new trade or re-educate yourself for a different career path. Going to school or taking classes at a public facility will subject you to further interaction with unknown individuals and increase the likelihood of being discovered. You may have to forego the life of an insurance salesman in exchange for that of a ranch hand or landscaper.

What will happen if you get caught trying to use fake documents as proof of identity? If you think the criminal charges you are trying to escape right now are bad, wait until you complicate matters by getting caught with identification obtained through illicit means. Not only will you be subjected to the sentence you were running from you will undoubtedly receive harsher recognition at the mercy of the federal judicial system when they hand down their sentence. What might have been a six month sentence spent sitting in the county lockup is now going to be a six year stint at a federal prison. While convicted felons of state run court systems do find it more difficult to land a respectable employment position within a successful company, those with a 'federal' tab in front of their felony status have almost no hope of being hired by anyone outside a criminal enterprise.

While there are several legitimate and worthwhile reasons for wanting to secure a new identity, many people do not take the time to think about all of the various aspects associated with this idea. Hundreds of people feel they could live a much better lifestyle if they could just give up on their current situation and start all over. They do not stop and consider that if they employ the same habits to the new persona, they will ultimately end up with the same dissatisfying results. You will never escape credit card debt if you cannot modify your shopping habits and exclude paying for everything with plastic. Yes, a new identity and credit history will clean the slate, but using the same spending and non-payment procedures as before is going to create another headache in the not too distant future.

One of the most overlooked areas that really warrant serious consideration, especially in this day and age is the medical history of the entire family unit. Have you thought about what might happen if you are involved in a life threatening accident? What if you develop a potentially fatal disease that requires a bone marrow transplant or an organ donor that is related? Your new identity might allow you the opportunity to enjoy a lifestyle you never had before; however it might also prevent you from enjoying life at all. Do you know what often happens to people who pass away and have no known next of kin? At best they are buried in a nondescript grave at a funeral attended by a handful of people they didn't know. In some cases, depending on region and population, John & Jane Doe end up being scavenged for useful organs or sold on the black market for medical studies and experiments.

Living a life based on lies is not an easy process for even the most talented among us. Hollywood actors spend countless hours, days, weeks and months rehearsing the roles they are assigned to play just to put 90 minutes of useable film on the big screen. Granted they are often depicting a character and everyone in the audience knows who they really are; however the attention to detail and effort to master the art of identity deception is the same. The best actors and actresses in the business are the ones that make the audience believe in the story no matter how illogical or insane it may seem.

They do not perfect this by using the same mannerisms that are associated with their true identity; they incorporate new tweaks, twists and turns to entice the viewer to relate to the character being portrayed. If you got a 'D' in Drama and Theater, then this is not going to be something you pull off easily.

Areas & Obstacles to Avoid

If you have made it to the point that your bags are packed and the new driver's license is in the back pocket, birth certificate and SSN are in an envelope tucked away in a safe place, the new identity has been established and you are about to leave the keys on the counter as you walk out the door, take one last look around. The only thing you should be taking out the door with you is the clothes on your back and the few unsentimental items you have in a carry bag. In order for your escape to be successful everything else should stay here. Read that again. Everything else should stay here. Nobody packs up their belongings and disappears, those people are trying to hide from something or somebody, they aren't really looking to start over, they are just looking for a new place to be found.

Once you leave your residence and put your new identity into play there is very little chance of turning back without being subject to criminal penalties under the law. Even if your intentions were for self-preservation or survival you could face punishment should you decide to expose the scam. Everything you have become familiar with needs to rest in this final place of your previous life. All of your hobbies and interests should change with your identity; this includes everything from fan support for a particular sports team to how you hold a cup of coffee. Nothing about the new you should mirror an aspect of the old you. The further you differentiate the two the greater your chance of pulling off the chameleon caper.

Not only should your mannerisms change but your aesthetic appearance should be altered as well. You don't need to run out and get reconstructive plastic surgery, just change little features about your look. If the old you had long hair and scruffy facial hair, consider going with a more modern buzz cut and either shave completely or keep the facial hair neat and trimmed. You would be surprised how well you can hide yourself in plain sight if you just change the angle of perception and how others view you. Change your hair color, clothing style, anything you can think of. Use over the counter items at your disposal. Color changing contact lenses can alter your appearance enough to cause even the most familiar family member to take a second look.

Stay away from areas people from your past were familiar with frequenting. If your poker buddies were famous for planning semi-annual 'business trips' to Las Vegas, then don't set up your new residence in Nevada. If your network of family and friends is wide spread across the entire country or over the whole planet such as would be the case with military dependents, then your choices of living locations may be severely limited. You will want to eliminate any place within approximately 100 hundred miles of a military installation, as these areas will pose the highest risk of you running across a long lost friend from the distant past you had completely forgotten about.

Avoid attending events, functions or other socially interactive environments that have the potential for attracting the attention of the police. You may have pulled the wool over the eyes of the state agencies responsible for issuing you copies of the documents you needed to get your new identity, but if you are arrested and fingerprinted, then the facets of your fallacy will soon fall apart. Be aware of your surroundings at all times and give serious consideration to what problems may occur.

If you are ever in an area and you hear the name of a person you associate with your past, it is time to move on. Do not sit idly by trying to eavesdrop on the conversation and find out more information. Leave the area immediately and consider it compromised. Any indication that your present is about to cross paths with your past means that you are not far enough away for safety. How do criminals get caught 90% percent of the time? They revisit or remain at the scene of the crime. The same can be said about people looking to pose as someone else. You will only get caught by being careless.

Do not assume you are safe and secure. Anything that casts doubt on your level of confidence should be cause for concern. Handle yourself accordingly and you can eliminate some of the worry.

Stay away from major metropolitan areas when conducting travel. This applies to bus stations, train depots and airports as well as car rental companies. These places represent the highest possibility of discovery. People from all walks of life travel on a daily basis, it has become second nature, no longer a simple luxury but in many cases a necessity. All it takes is for Joe Blow, the guy that you met at a college frat party 20 years ago, to start calling out your real name in a crowded airport before your new persona is null and void.

Eliminate the urge to recreate online social network accounts. You do not want to be found for one reason or another, so the internet is now your enemy is this regard. The technology employed on these social web sites can be used to track individuals that simply visit the page of another person. Even with a bogus name and new identity an online equivalent can lead to discovery. Do not make purchases online using your new identity as it will establish a paper trail in cyber space. The harder you make it for someone to associate the new you with the old you the easier it will be to make new associates believe in the image you are selling.

A great rule of thumb to live by when surviving under a new identity situation is to always expect the unexpected. That may sound like the oldest cliché in the book but it applies to this type of scenario on a daily basis. You should never assume that your new identity is rock solid and cannot be brought to the public's attention either inadvertently or on purpose. Ask yourself; "Would the old me do this?" If the answer is 'yes,' find something else to do. Chance is only something that should be associated with gambling and the last thing you want to place a wager on is how well your new identity is going to hold up.

Your new alter ego should be the anti-thesis of your current persona. It should be the Jeckyll to your Hyde, an image nobody would expect in the least of being in anyway affiliated with the other. Your own mother should be able to walk past you in the supermarket without getting a gleam of recognition in her eye.

You may find the information at http://www.bombshock.com/disappearing-and-living-free very helpful and worthy or reading. Obtaining a new identity usually involves wanting to remain off the grid and the site listed above has some very informative literature regarding this aspect of the situation.

Leaving Your Past Behind

Depending on your circumstances leaving your loved ones behind is going to be the hardest part of living under a new identity. All too often it is the desire to reconnect with the friends and family from the past that causes deceptive individuals to attempt to circumvent living under a fake name. The urge to let the grieving know you are okay can be overwhelming. If you have any hope of maintaining the integrity of your new identity, then you will have to eliminate this desire at all costs.

Do not take any pictures of people from your past with you into the new lifestyle. These photos can be very difficult to explain; especially to new associates should they be seen. They can also be used to establish a logical and legitimate connection between you and the person that supposedly disappeared. They are a paper trail to the past that can cripple the present in a matter of moments. The only images you should take are mental memories.

Most people in the modern era have a cell phone of one sort or another. Get rid of it. Leave it on the counter with the keys or find a way to dismantle and destroy it. Many of these devices have the capability of being traced for location; if you carry it on your person you are using a personal tracking device. If you absolutely have to have a cell phone as part of your new identity, then purchase one at full retail and initiate a month to month payment plan for service or buy an over the counter equivalent that is not tied into the corporate cellular industry.

Do not save, store or in any way, shape or form, maintain methods of contacting people from your past. Get rid of their phone numbers, their email addresses, social networking accounts or anything that might allow you in some way to make an errant mistake of this nature. Do not ever return to your last known place of existence. As a matter of fact it would be wise to eliminate that entire section of country from any future plans.

Make peace with everything in your present, soon to be past. Do not leave any lingering doubts or un-snipped strings attached. Successfully living in secrecy requires a 'you vs. the world' mentality. You cannot rely on help from former friends and family members, nor should you expect it from new acquaintances. Be completely comfortable and confident in your decision to dive into a new identity. Once your roller coaster reaches that final peak and pushes over the lip, you are going to be along for the ride, no matter how good, bad or ugly it ends up.

If your time away from reality will be temporary, then you might want to have a re-entry strategy as well as an exit plan. Most criminal charges carry a statute of limitations with them, making it impossible for the accused to be prosecuted after a predetermined amount of time has passed. If your exit strategy involves keeping a low profile approach, then the re-entry plan should also involve a modicum of discretion. You don't necessarily want to surprise everyone and alert the authorities that you are back in the area. Even if they can't prosecute you for past activity they can make life in the area hell to deal with.

If an emergency situation arises that mandates making contact a necessity for sustaining the life of another make the necessary arrangements to facilitate contact from a location that is not where you have established your new residence and only under extreme circumstances.

ALL RIGHTS RESERVED. No part of this publication may be reproduced or transmitted in any form whatsoever, electronic, or mechanical, including photocopying, recording, or by any informational storage or retrieval system without express written, dated and signed permission from the author.

DISCLAIMER AND/OR LEGAL NOTICES: Every effort has been made to accurately represent this book and it's potential. Results vary with every individual, and your results may or may not be different from those depicted. No promises, guarantees or warranties, whether stated or implied, have been made that you will produce any specific result from this book. Your efforts are individual and unique, and may vary from those shown. Your success depends on your efforts, background and motivation.

The material in this publication is provided for educational and informational purposes only and is not intended as medical advice. The information contained in this book should not be used to diagnose or treat any illness, metabolic disorder, disease or health problem. Always consult your physician or health care provider before beginning any nutrition or exercise program. Use of the programs, advice, and information contained in this book is at the sole choice and risk of the reader.

www.ingramcontent.com/pod-product-compliance
Lightning Source LLC
Chambersburg PA
CBHW061224180526
45170CB00003B/1140